50 Lemon or Garlic Dishes

By: Kelly Johnson

Table of Contents

- Garlic Butter Shrimp Scampi
- Lemon Herb Roasted Chicken
- Garlic Parmesan Crusted Salmon
- Lemon Ricotta Pancakes
- Garlic Butter Steak Bites
- Lemon Dill Baked Cod
- Roasted Garlic Mashed Potatoes
- Lemon Basil Pesto Pasta
- Garlic Confit with Olive Oil
- Lemon Garlic Roasted Asparagus
- Garlic Butter Lobster Tails
- Lemon Pepper Crusted Tilapia
- Garlic Honey Glazed Chicken Thighs
- Lemon Garlic Hummus
- Garlic Butter Mushrooms
- Lemon Herb Quinoa Salad
- Garlic Parmesan Roasted Broccoli
- Lemon Butter Scallops
- Roasted Garlic Tomato Soup
- Lemon Olive Oil Cake
- Garlic and Rosemary Roasted Potatoes
- Lemon Garlic Marinated Olives
- Garlic Butter Naan Bread
- Lemon Zested Cheesecake Bars
- Garlic Spinach and Ricotta Stuffed Shells
- Lemon Meringue Pie
- Garlic Roasted Brussels Sprouts
- Lemon Chia Seed Pudding
- Garlic Herb Butter Basted Ribeye
- Lemon Poppy Seed Muffins
- Garlic Ginger Stir-Fried Shrimp
- Lemon Garlic Grilled Lamb Chops
- Roasted Garlic Aioli Dip
- Lemon Infused Olive Oil Dressing
- Garlic Cream Cheese Stuffed Jalapeños

- Lemon Sorbet with Mint
- Garlic Parmesan Breadsticks
- Lemon and Thyme Roasted Duck
- Garlic Chili Oil Noodles
- Lemon Caper Chicken Piccata
- Garlic Butter Baked Oysters
- Lemon Honey Glazed Carrots
- Garlic Roasted Cauliflower Steaks
- Lemon Dill Yogurt Sauce
- Garlic and Lemon Infused Rice Pilaf
- Lemon and Garlic Braised Artichokes
- Garlic and Herb Focaccia Bread
- Lemon Basil Shrimp Risotto
- Garlic Roasted Chickpeas
- Lemon Butter Poached Lobster

Garlic Butter Shrimp Scampi

Ingredients:

- 1/2 lb shrimp, peeled and deveined
- 2 tbsp butter
- 3 cloves garlic, minced
- 1/2 cup white wine (or chicken broth)
- 1 tbsp lemon juice
- 1/4 tsp red pepper flakes
- 1 tbsp parsley, chopped
- 8 oz linguine or spaghetti

Instructions:

1. Cook pasta according to package instructions; drain and set aside.
2. In a pan, melt butter and sauté garlic for 1 minute.
3. Add shrimp, cooking for 2 minutes per side.
4. Pour in white wine, lemon juice, and red pepper flakes; simmer for 2 minutes.
5. Toss in pasta and parsley before serving.

Lemon Herb Roasted Chicken

Ingredients:

- 1 whole chicken (3-4 lbs)
- 3 tbsp butter, melted
- 2 tbsp lemon juice
- 1 tbsp fresh rosemary, chopped
- 1 tbsp fresh thyme, chopped
- 4 cloves garlic, minced
- 1 tsp salt
- 1/2 tsp black pepper

Instructions:

1. Preheat oven to 400°F (200°C).
2. Mix butter, lemon juice, herbs, garlic, salt, and pepper.
3. Rub mixture under the skin and on top of the chicken.
4. Roast for 1 hour and 15 minutes, basting occasionally, until golden brown.
5. Let rest for 10 minutes before carving.

Garlic Parmesan Crusted Salmon

Ingredients:

- 2 salmon fillets
- 2 tbsp butter, melted
- 2 cloves garlic, minced
- 1/4 cup grated Parmesan cheese
- 1/4 cup breadcrumbs
- 1 tbsp parsley, chopped
- 1/2 tsp lemon zest

Instructions:

1. Preheat oven to 400°F (200°C).
2. Mix butter, garlic, Parmesan, breadcrumbs, parsley, and lemon zest.
3. Spread mixture on salmon and bake for 12–15 minutes.

Lemon Ricotta Pancakes

Ingredients:

- 1 cup all-purpose flour
- 1 tbsp sugar
- 1/2 tsp baking soda
- 1/4 tsp salt
- 3/4 cup ricotta cheese
- 1/2 cup milk
- 2 eggs
- 2 tbsp lemon juice
- 1 tsp lemon zest

Instructions:

1. Mix dry ingredients in one bowl and wet ingredients in another.
2. Combine both until just mixed.
3. Cook pancakes on a greased skillet for 2 minutes per side.

Garlic Butter Steak Bites

Ingredients:

- 1 lb sirloin steak, cubed
- 2 tbsp butter
- 3 cloves garlic, minced
- 1 tsp salt
- 1/2 tsp black pepper
- 1 tsp parsley, chopped

Instructions:

1. Heat butter in a pan over high heat.
2. Sear steak bites for 2 minutes per side.
3. Add garlic, cooking for 30 seconds.
4. Garnish with parsley before serving.

Lemon Dill Baked Cod

Ingredients:

- 2 cod fillets
- 2 tbsp olive oil
- 1 tbsp lemon juice
- 1 tsp fresh dill, chopped
- 2 cloves garlic, minced
- 1/2 tsp salt
- 1/4 tsp black pepper

Instructions:

1. Preheat oven to 375°F (190°C).
2. Mix olive oil, lemon juice, dill, garlic, salt, and pepper.
3. Coat cod fillets with mixture and bake for 12–15 minutes.

Roasted Garlic Mashed Potatoes

Ingredients:

- 4 large potatoes, peeled and cubed
- 1 whole head garlic, roasted
- 1/2 cup heavy cream
- 3 tbsp butter
- 1/2 tsp salt
- 1/4 tsp black pepper

Instructions:

1. Boil potatoes until tender, then drain.
2. Mash potatoes with roasted garlic, cream, butter, salt, and pepper.

Lemon Basil Pesto Pasta

Ingredients:

- 8 oz pasta
- 2 cups fresh basil
- 1/2 cup Parmesan cheese, grated
- 1/3 cup olive oil
- 2 cloves garlic
- 1 tbsp lemon juice
- 1/4 tsp salt

Instructions:

1. Blend basil, Parmesan, olive oil, garlic, lemon juice, and salt into a smooth pesto.
2. Toss with cooked pasta and serve.

Garlic Confit with Olive Oil

Ingredients:

- 1 cup garlic cloves, peeled
- 1 cup olive oil

Instructions:

1. Simmer garlic in olive oil on low heat for 30–40 minutes until soft.
2. Store in an airtight container in the fridge.

Lemon Garlic Roasted Asparagus

Ingredients:

- 1 bunch asparagus, trimmed
- 2 tbsp olive oil
- 2 cloves garlic, minced
- 1 tbsp lemon juice
- 1/4 tsp salt

Instructions:

1. Preheat oven to 400°F (200°C).
2. Toss asparagus with olive oil, garlic, lemon juice, and salt.
3. Roast for 12–15 minutes.

Garlic Butter Lobster Tails

Ingredients:

- 2 lobster tails
- 2 tbsp butter, melted
- 2 cloves garlic, minced
- 1 tbsp lemon juice
- 1 tsp parsley, chopped
- 1/2 tsp paprika
- Salt & black pepper

Instructions:

1. Preheat oven to 400°F (200°C). Cut lobster tails down the center and pull the meat slightly out.
2. Mix butter, garlic, lemon juice, paprika, salt, and pepper.
3. Brush mixture over lobster meat and bake for 10–12 minutes, basting once.
4. Garnish with parsley before serving.

Lemon Pepper Crusted Tilapia

Ingredients:

- 2 tilapia fillets
- 1/2 cup breadcrumbs
- 1 tsp lemon zest
- 1/2 tsp black pepper
- 1/2 tsp salt
- 1 tbsp olive oil

Instructions:

1. Preheat oven to 375°F (190°C).
2. Mix breadcrumbs, lemon zest, pepper, and salt.
3. Brush tilapia with olive oil and coat with breadcrumb mixture.
4. Bake for 12–15 minutes until golden brown.

Garlic Honey Glazed Chicken Thighs

Ingredients:

- 4 bone-in, skin-on chicken thighs
- 2 tbsp butter
- 3 cloves garlic, minced
- 2 tbsp honey
- 1 tbsp soy sauce
- 1/2 tsp black pepper
- 1/2 tsp salt

Instructions:

1. Preheat oven to 375°F (190°C).
2. Sear chicken thighs skin-side down until crispy, about 4 minutes.
3. In a saucepan, melt butter and mix in garlic, honey, soy sauce, salt, and pepper.
4. Brush sauce over chicken and bake for 25 minutes.

Lemon Garlic Hummus

Ingredients:

- 1 can (14 oz) chickpeas, drained
- 2 tbsp tahini
- 2 tbsp lemon juice
- 2 cloves garlic
- 1/4 cup olive oil
- 1/2 tsp salt

Instructions:

1. Blend chickpeas, tahini, lemon juice, garlic, and salt until smooth.
2. Slowly drizzle in olive oil while blending.
3. Serve with pita bread or vegetables.

Garlic Butter Mushrooms

Ingredients:

- 2 cups mushrooms, halved
- 2 tbsp butter
- 3 cloves garlic, minced
- 1 tbsp fresh parsley, chopped
- 1/2 tsp salt
- 1/4 tsp black pepper

Instructions:

1. Melt butter in a pan over medium heat.
2. Sauté mushrooms for 5 minutes.
3. Add garlic, salt, and pepper, cooking for another 2 minutes.
4. Garnish with parsley before serving.

Lemon Herb Quinoa Salad

Ingredients:

- 1 cup quinoa, cooked
- 1/2 cup cherry tomatoes, halved
- 1/4 cup cucumber, diced
- 2 tbsp lemon juice
- 1 tbsp olive oil
- 1 tbsp fresh parsley, chopped
- 1/2 tsp salt

Instructions:

1. Mix quinoa, tomatoes, and cucumber in a bowl.
2. Whisk lemon juice, olive oil, salt, and parsley.
3. Toss salad with dressing and serve.

Garlic Parmesan Roasted Broccoli

Ingredients:

- 2 cups broccoli florets
- 2 tbsp olive oil
- 2 cloves garlic, minced
- 1/4 cup Parmesan cheese, grated
- 1/2 tsp salt
- 1/4 tsp black pepper

Instructions:

1. Preheat oven to 400°F (200°C).
2. Toss broccoli with olive oil, garlic, salt, and pepper.
3. Roast for 15 minutes, then sprinkle with Parmesan.
4. Bake for another 5 minutes until golden.

Lemon Butter Scallops

Ingredients:

- 6 large sea scallops
- 2 tbsp butter
- 1 tbsp lemon juice
- 1 clove garlic, minced
- 1/2 tsp salt
- 1/4 tsp black pepper

Instructions:

1. Pat scallops dry and season with salt and pepper.
2. Heat butter in a pan and sear scallops for 2 minutes per side.
3. Stir in garlic and lemon juice, cooking for another 30 seconds.
4. Serve immediately.

Roasted Garlic Tomato Soup

Ingredients:

- 4 tomatoes, chopped
- 1 whole head garlic, roasted
- 1 small onion, chopped
- 2 cups vegetable broth
- 1/2 cup heavy cream
- 1 tbsp olive oil
- 1/2 tsp salt
- 1/4 tsp black pepper

Instructions:

1. Roast tomatoes and garlic at 375°F (190°C) for 25 minutes.
2. Sauté onions in olive oil, then blend with roasted tomatoes and garlic.
3. Simmer with broth, salt, and pepper for 10 minutes.
4. Stir in heavy cream before serving.

Lemon Olive Oil Cake

Ingredients:

- 1 1/2 cups all-purpose flour
- 3/4 cup sugar
- 1/2 cup olive oil
- 1/2 cup milk
- 2 eggs
- 1 tbsp lemon juice
- 1 tsp lemon zest
- 1/2 tsp baking powder
- 1/4 tsp salt

Instructions:

1. Preheat oven to 350°F (175°C).
2. Whisk flour, sugar, baking powder, and salt.
3. Mix in olive oil, milk, eggs, lemon juice, and zest.
4. Pour into a greased pan and bake for 30 minutes.

Garlic and Rosemary Roasted Potatoes

Ingredients:

- 2 lbs baby potatoes, halved
- 2 tbsp olive oil
- 3 cloves garlic, minced
- 1 tsp fresh rosemary, chopped
- 1/2 tsp salt
- 1/4 tsp black pepper

Instructions:

1. Preheat oven to 400°F (200°C).
2. Toss potatoes with olive oil, garlic, rosemary, salt, and pepper.
3. Roast for 35–40 minutes until crispy.

Lemon Garlic Marinated Olives

Ingredients:

- 1 cup mixed olives
- 2 tbsp olive oil
- 2 cloves garlic, minced
- 1 tsp lemon zest
- 1 tbsp lemon juice
- 1/2 tsp red pepper flakes
- 1 tsp fresh thyme

Instructions:

1. In a small bowl, mix olive oil, garlic, lemon zest, lemon juice, red pepper flakes, and thyme.
2. Toss olives in the marinade and let sit for at least 30 minutes before serving.

Garlic Butter Naan Bread

Ingredients:

- 2 cups all-purpose flour
- 1/2 cup Greek yogurt
- 1/2 cup warm water
- 1 tsp baking powder
- 1/2 tsp salt
- 2 tbsp butter, melted
- 2 cloves garlic, minced

Instructions:

1. Mix flour, yogurt, water, baking powder, and salt into a soft dough. Let rest for 30 minutes.
2. Divide into small balls, roll out into rounds, and cook on a hot skillet for 2 minutes per side.
3. Mix melted butter with garlic and brush over warm naan.

Lemon Zested Cheesecake Bars

Ingredients:

- **For Crust:**
    - 1 1/2 cups graham cracker crumbs
    - 1/4 cup melted butter
    - 2 tbsp sugar
- **For Filling:**
    - 16 oz cream cheese, softened
    - 1/2 cup sugar
    - 1 tbsp lemon zest
    - 2 tbsp lemon juice
    - 2 eggs

Instructions:

1. Preheat oven to 350°F (175°C).
2. Mix crust ingredients, press into a baking dish, and bake for 8 minutes.
3. Beat cream cheese, sugar, lemon zest, and lemon juice until smooth. Mix in eggs.
4. Pour over crust and bake for 25 minutes. Chill before slicing.

Garlic Spinach and Ricotta Stuffed Shells

Ingredients:

- 12 jumbo pasta shells
- 1 cup ricotta cheese
- 1/2 cup spinach, chopped
- 2 cloves garlic, minced
- 1/2 cup Parmesan cheese, grated
- 1 egg
- 1 cup marinara sauce

Instructions:

1. Preheat oven to 375°F (190°C).
2. Cook pasta shells according to package instructions.
3. Mix ricotta, spinach, garlic, Parmesan, and egg.
4. Stuff shells with filling, place in a baking dish, and top with marinara sauce.
5. Bake for 20 minutes.

Lemon Meringue Pie

Ingredients:

- **For Crust:**
    - 1 1/2 cups graham cracker crumbs
    - 1/4 cup melted butter
- **For Lemon Filling:**
    - 1 cup sugar
    - 1/4 cup cornstarch
    - 1 cup water
    - 1/2 cup lemon juice
    - 1 tbsp lemon zest
    - 4 egg yolks
    - 2 tbsp butter
- **For Meringue:**
    - 4 egg whites
    - 1/4 cup sugar

Instructions:

1. Preheat oven to 350°F (175°C). Mix crust ingredients, press into a pie pan, and bake for 8 minutes.
2. In a saucepan, whisk sugar, cornstarch, water, lemon juice, and zest over medium heat.
3. Whisk in egg yolks and butter until thickened. Pour into crust.
4. Whip egg whites and sugar until stiff peaks form. Spread over filling.
5. Bake for 10 minutes until golden.

Garlic Roasted Brussels Sprouts

Ingredients:

- 2 cups Brussels sprouts, halved
- 2 tbsp olive oil
- 3 cloves garlic, minced
- 1/2 tsp salt
- 1/4 tsp black pepper

Instructions:

1. Preheat oven to 400°F (200°C).
2. Toss Brussels sprouts with olive oil, garlic, salt, and pepper.
3. Roast for 25 minutes until crispy.

Lemon Chia Seed Pudding

Ingredients:

- 1 cup almond milk
- 1/4 cup chia seeds
- 1 tbsp honey
- 1 tbsp lemon juice
- 1 tsp lemon zest

Instructions:

1. Mix all ingredients in a jar.
2. Let sit in the fridge for at least 4 hours, stirring once.

Garlic Herb Butter Basted Ribeye

Ingredients:

- 1 ribeye steak
- 2 tbsp butter
- 2 cloves garlic, minced
- 1 tsp fresh rosemary, chopped
- 1 tsp fresh thyme, chopped
- Salt & black pepper

Instructions:

1. Season steak with salt and pepper. Sear in a hot skillet for 3 minutes per side.
2. Reduce heat, add butter, garlic, rosemary, and thyme. Baste steak for 1 minute.
3. Rest for 5 minutes before serving.

Lemon Poppy Seed Muffins

Ingredients:

- 2 cups all-purpose flour
- 3/4 cup sugar
- 1 tbsp poppy seeds
- 1 tsp baking powder
- 1/2 tsp baking soda
- 1/2 cup milk
- 1/2 cup Greek yogurt
- 1/4 cup melted butter
- 2 tbsp lemon juice
- 1 tbsp lemon zest
- 1 egg

Instructions:

1. Preheat oven to 375°F (190°C).
2. Mix dry ingredients in one bowl and wet ingredients in another.
3. Combine both and spoon into muffin tins.
4. Bake for 18–20 minutes.

Garlic Ginger Stir-Fried Shrimp

Ingredients:

- 1/2 lb shrimp, peeled and deveined
- 1 tbsp soy sauce
- 1 tbsp sesame oil
- 2 cloves garlic, minced
- 1 tsp ginger, minced
- 1/2 tsp red pepper flakes

Instructions:

1. Heat sesame oil in a pan. Add garlic and ginger, cooking for 30 seconds.
2. Add shrimp and soy sauce, stir-frying for 3 minutes.
3. Sprinkle with red pepper flakes and serve.

Lemon Garlic Grilled Lamb Chops

Ingredients:

- 4 lamb chops
- 2 tbsp olive oil
- 2 cloves garlic, minced
- 1 tbsp lemon juice
- 1 tsp lemon zest
- 1 tsp fresh rosemary, chopped
- 1/2 tsp salt
- 1/4 tsp black pepper

Instructions:

1. Mix olive oil, garlic, lemon juice, zest, rosemary, salt, and pepper.
2. Marinate lamb chops for at least 30 minutes.
3. Grill over medium-high heat for 3–4 minutes per side.
4. Let rest for 5 minutes before serving.

Roasted Garlic Aioli Dip

Ingredients:

- 1 whole head garlic
- 1/2 cup mayonnaise
- 1 tbsp lemon juice
- 1 tsp Dijon mustard
- 1/4 tsp salt
- 1/4 tsp black pepper

Instructions:

1. Roast garlic at 400°F (200°C) for 30 minutes.
2. Squeeze out softened garlic and mash into a paste.
3. Mix with mayonnaise, lemon juice, mustard, salt, and pepper.
4. Chill before serving.

Lemon Infused Olive Oil Dressing

Ingredients:

- 1/2 cup olive oil
- 2 tbsp lemon juice
- 1 tsp lemon zest
- 1 tsp honey
- 1/2 tsp Dijon mustard
- 1/2 tsp salt
- 1/4 tsp black pepper

Instructions:

1. Whisk all ingredients together until emulsified.
2. Store in a jar and shake before serving.

Garlic Cream Cheese Stuffed Jalapeños

Ingredients:

- 6 jalapeños, halved and deseeded
- 1/2 cup cream cheese
- 2 cloves garlic, minced
- 1/4 cup shredded cheddar cheese
- 1/2 tsp salt
- 1/4 tsp black pepper

Instructions:

1. Preheat oven to 375°F (190°C).
2. Mix cream cheese, garlic, cheddar, salt, and pepper.
3. Fill jalapeño halves with mixture and bake for 15 minutes.

Lemon Sorbet with Mint

Ingredients:

- 1 cup lemon juice
- 1 cup water
- 3/4 cup sugar
- 1 tsp lemon zest
- 1 tbsp fresh mint, chopped

Instructions:

1. Heat water and sugar until dissolved, then cool.
2. Mix with lemon juice and zest.
3. Freeze, stirring every 30 minutes until set.
4. Garnish with mint before serving.

Garlic Parmesan Breadsticks

Ingredients:

- 2 cups all-purpose flour
- 1 packet (2 1/4 tsp) yeast
- 3/4 cup warm water
- 1 tbsp olive oil
- 1/2 tsp salt
- 2 tbsp butter, melted
- 2 cloves garlic, minced
- 1/4 cup Parmesan cheese, grated

Instructions:

1. Mix flour, yeast, warm water, olive oil, and salt into a dough. Let rise for 1 hour.
2. Roll into breadsticks and bake at 375°F (190°C) for 12 minutes.
3. Brush with butter, garlic, and Parmesan before serving.

Lemon and Thyme Roasted Duck

Ingredients:

- 1 whole duck
- 2 tbsp butter, melted
- 1 tbsp lemon juice
- 1 tsp lemon zest
- 1 tsp fresh thyme, chopped
- 2 cloves garlic, minced
- 1/2 tsp salt
- 1/4 tsp black pepper

Instructions:

1. Preheat oven to 375°F (190°C).
2. Mix butter, lemon juice, zest, thyme, garlic, salt, and pepper.
3. Rub all over the duck and roast for 1 hour, basting occasionally.

Garlic Chili Oil Noodles

Ingredients:

- 8 oz noodles
- 2 tbsp sesame oil
- 2 cloves garlic, minced
- 1 tsp red chili flakes
- 1 tbsp soy sauce
- 1 tsp rice vinegar
- 1/2 tsp sugar

Instructions:

1. Cook noodles and drain.
2. Heat sesame oil, garlic, and chili flakes in a pan for 1 minute.
3. Mix in soy sauce, rice vinegar, and sugar. Toss with noodles.

Lemon Caper Chicken Piccata

Ingredients:

- 2 chicken breasts, pounded thin
- 1/2 cup flour
- 1 tbsp olive oil
- 1/2 cup chicken broth
- 1/4 cup lemon juice
- 2 tbsp capers
- 2 tbsp butter

Instructions:

1. Dredge chicken in flour and sear in olive oil for 4 minutes per side.
2. Add broth, lemon juice, and capers, simmering for 5 minutes.
3. Stir in butter before serving.

Garlic Butter Baked Oysters

Ingredients:

- 6 fresh oysters, shucked
- 2 tbsp butter, melted
- 2 cloves garlic, minced
- 1 tbsp parsley, chopped
- 1 tbsp Parmesan cheese, grated
- 1/2 tsp lemon juice

Instructions:

1. Preheat oven to 400°F (200°C).
2. Mix butter, garlic, parsley, Parmesan, and lemon juice.
3. Spoon onto oysters and bake for 10 minutes.

Lemon Honey Glazed Carrots

Ingredients:

- 2 cups baby carrots
- 2 tbsp butter
- 1 tbsp honey
- 1 tbsp lemon juice
- 1/2 tsp lemon zest
- 1/4 tsp salt
- 1/4 tsp black pepper

Instructions:

1. Steam or boil carrots until tender, about 5 minutes.
2. In a pan, melt butter and stir in honey, lemon juice, and zest.
3. Add carrots, tossing to coat, and cook for 2 more minutes.

Garlic Roasted Cauliflower Steaks

Ingredients:

- 1 large head cauliflower, sliced into 1-inch steaks
- 2 tbsp olive oil
- 2 cloves garlic, minced
- 1/2 tsp salt
- 1/4 tsp black pepper
- 1/2 tsp smoked paprika

Instructions:

1. Preheat oven to 400°F (200°C).
2. Brush cauliflower with olive oil and sprinkle with garlic, salt, pepper, and paprika.
3. Roast for 25 minutes, flipping halfway through.

Lemon Dill Yogurt Sauce

Ingredients:

- 1/2 cup Greek yogurt
- 1 tbsp lemon juice
- 1 tsp lemon zest
- 1 tbsp fresh dill, chopped
- 1 clove garlic, minced
- 1/4 tsp salt

Instructions:

1. Mix all ingredients in a bowl.
2. Refrigerate for at least 15 minutes before serving.

Garlic and Lemon Infused Rice Pilaf

Ingredients:

- 1 cup basmati rice
- 2 cups chicken or vegetable broth
- 2 cloves garlic, minced
- 1 tbsp lemon juice
- 1/2 tsp lemon zest
- 1 tbsp olive oil
- 1/4 tsp salt

Instructions:

1. Heat olive oil in a pan and sauté garlic for 1 minute.
2. Add rice and toast for 2 minutes.
3. Pour in broth, lemon juice, zest, and salt. Bring to a boil, cover, and simmer for 15 minutes.

Lemon and Garlic Braised Artichokes

Ingredients:

- 2 large artichokes, trimmed and halved
- 2 tbsp olive oil
- 3 cloves garlic, minced
- 1 cup vegetable broth
- 2 tbsp lemon juice
- 1/2 tsp salt
- 1/4 tsp black pepper

Instructions:

1. Heat olive oil in a pan and sauté garlic for 1 minute.
2. Add artichokes, cut side down, and brown for 3 minutes.
3. Pour in broth and lemon juice, cover, and simmer for 25 minutes.

Garlic and Herb Focaccia Bread

Ingredients:

- 3 1/2 cups all-purpose flour
- 1 packet (2 1/4 tsp) yeast
- 1 cup warm water
- 1/4 cup olive oil
- 3 cloves garlic, minced
- 1 tsp fresh rosemary, chopped
- 1/2 tsp salt

Instructions:

1. Mix flour, yeast, warm water, and salt into a dough. Let rise for 1 hour.
2. Flatten onto a greased baking sheet, pressing dimples into the dough.
3. Brush with olive oil, garlic, and rosemary.
4. Bake at 375°F (190°C) for 20 minutes.

Lemon Basil Shrimp Risotto

Ingredients:

- 1 cup Arborio rice
- 2 1/2 cups chicken or seafood broth
- 1/2 lb shrimp, peeled and deveined
- 1/4 cup white wine
- 2 tbsp butter
- 2 cloves garlic, minced
- 1 tbsp lemon juice
- 1 tsp lemon zest
- 1 tbsp fresh basil, chopped

Instructions:

1. Sauté garlic and rice in butter for 2 minutes.
2. Deglaze with white wine, then gradually add broth, stirring continuously.
3. Once rice is creamy, add shrimp, lemon juice, zest, and basil.
4. Cook until shrimp are pink, about 3 minutes.

Garlic Roasted Chickpeas

Ingredients:

- 1 can (14 oz) chickpeas, drained and patted dry
- 2 tbsp olive oil
- 2 cloves garlic, minced
- 1/2 tsp salt
- 1/4 tsp smoked paprika
- 1/4 tsp black pepper

Instructions:

1. Preheat oven to 400°F (200°C).
2. Toss chickpeas with olive oil, garlic, salt, paprika, and pepper.
3. Roast for 25 minutes, shaking the pan halfway through.

Lemon Butter Poached Lobster

Ingredients:

- 2 lobster tails, shells removed
- 4 tbsp butter
- 1 tbsp lemon juice
- 1/2 tsp lemon zest
- 1 clove garlic, minced
- 1/4 tsp salt
- 1/4 tsp black pepper

Instructions:

1. Melt butter in a pan over low heat and add lemon juice, zest, garlic, salt, and pepper.
2. Gently poach lobster tails in butter for 5–6 minutes, spooning butter over them.
3. Serve immediately.